OXFORD'S WORKING PAST

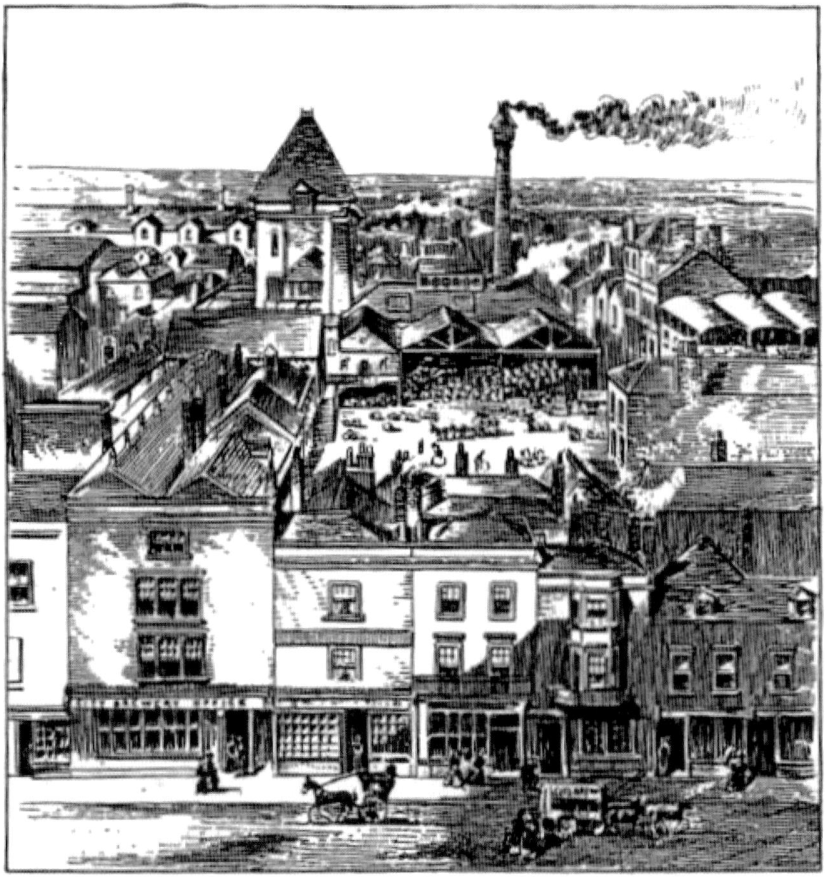

Hanley's City Brewery, which occupied a substantial area bordered by Pembroke Street, St. Ebbe's Street, and Queen Street (at the bottom of the picture). In the Victorian period Oxford's industrial buildings were not clustered together in out-of-town industrial estates as they are today, but instead were often cheek-by-jowl with domestic houses and with shops in the centre of the city. Their large sites had an important effect on the topography of Oxford; their many chimneys had a significant impact on the famous skyline; and the smells and noise that they produced were an everyday part of many citizen's lives. Image from Alfred Barnard's *The Noted Breweries of Great Britain and Ireland*, vol. 3 (1891), p. 440.

OXFORD'S WORKING PAST

Walking Tours of Victorian and Edwardian Industrial Buildings

LIZ WOOLLEY

HUXLEY SCIENTIFIC PRESS
OXFORD

Published by Huxley Scientific Press
35 Marston Street, Oxford OX4 1JU, UK
www.huxleyscientific.com

First published 2012

ISBN-13: 978-0-9522671-7-1

Typeset in Monotype Plantin by the Geometric Press, Oxford
Cover design by Geoff Ager: geoff.ager@ntlworld.com
Maps by Cath d'Alton: cathdaltonhome@btinternet.com
Printed by Information Press, Eynsham, Oxford

Foreword by Malcolm Graham

The words 'Oxford' and 'heritage' are virtually synonymous, but rarely do we consider local industry as part of that heritage. In Victorian times, when a Parliamentary Committee asked an Oxford alderman whether the city had any manufactures, he replied: 'Oh, yes, sir! We have two, Parsons and Sausages.' In 1851, Samuel Sidney noted appreciatively that Oxford was 'so decorously clean, so spotlessly free from the smoke of engines and the roar of machinery'. By comparison with major industrial centres, Oxford was, of course, a peaceful place, but all around the city there were business premises where men, women, and children were hard at work.

Oxford might have become a major manufacturing centre long before William Morris began making cars at Cowley in 1913. In 1546, Christ Church leased the remains of Osney Abbey to William Stumpe, a Malmesbury clothier, anticipating that he would 'fynd worke for [2,000] persons from tyme to tyme, if they may be gotten, that will do their worke well continually in clothemakyng, for the succour of the Cytye of Oxenford and the contrey abowt yt.' That scheme came to nothing, as in 1865 did a proposal by the Great Western Railway Company to build carriage workshops near the railway station. The city and a few university figures welcomed the GWR scheme for the prosperity it would bring and St. John's College happily anticipated an increased demand for artisan housing on its Oxford estates. The university was generally opposed, however, fearing that the development would interfere with undergraduate discipline and endanger Oxford's distinctive character. The GWR eventually opted to build the workshops at Swindon, and the threat of industrial smoke billowing across the city was averted.

Until the twentieth century, the university was the key driver of Oxford's economy. Local tradesmen flourished by supplying commodities to colleges and undergraduates, and some gained a wider reputation by providing delicacies such as Oxford sausages or Oxford marmalade. Booksellers—including Blackwell's since 1879—have for generations prospered from university custom. The first book was printed in Oxford in 1478 and the University Press has a continuous history from 1585. After moving to Walton Street in 1830, it became a substantial local employer with a workforce of 278 by 1883. Major building firms flourished by erecting, restoring, and maintaining the ever-growing estate of university and college buildings. University demand also encouraged the development of specialist crafts such as boatbuilding, clockmaking, bespoke shoemaking, even the manufacture of cricket bats and balls.

Oxford was also a county town, the Christminster of Thomas Hardy's *Jude the Obscure*, and, increasingly, 'a residential resort to which a great many are attracted who have no ostensible connection with the University at all'. These roles encouraged other enterprises, familiar in all urban centres—a cattle market, bakeries, breweries and malthouses, iron foundries, clothing factories, waterworks, gas and electricity works, railways and tramways. Some of these businesses became important employers and they could be unwelcome neighbours, but their polluting effects were less evident in the ancient heart of the city.

The closure of Morrell's Lion Brewery in 2002 marked the end of an era in Oxford and you can no longer experience the intriguing smell of hops wafting across the city centre. What you can still do, of course, is to explore those sites and buildings which reveal Oxford's working past, something I've enjoyed for over forty years! I therefore very much welcome this well-illustrated booklet, which both guides you to the key sites and explains the processes that were carried on there. As a bonus, it also offers three enjoyable walks through less familiar parts of Oxford.

Malcolm Graham
Oxford
March 2012

Acknowledgements

The author thanks the following for their help with historical research and with the preparation of the manuscript: Malcolm Graham, Chris Day, Chris Hall, Geoffrey Tyack, Helen Drury, Simon Wenham, Abigail Lloyd, and Pete Lock.

The Greening Lamborn Trust

The author and publisher are grateful to the Greening Lamborn Trust for a generous grant towards the publication of this booklet. The trust's objective is to promote public interest in the history, architecture, old photographs, and heraldry of Oxford and its neighbourhood by supporting publications and other media that create access to them.

Preface

Not many of us would think of Oxford as 'industrial': the Industrial Revolution more or less passed the city by and in 1850 its population was still one of small tradesmen, shopkeepers, and servants, heavily dependent on the university. However, as Oxford expanded rapidly in the later nineteenth century—and as real wages rose and the mass media encouraged interest in manufactured commodities—the demand for gas, electricity, clean water, and consumer goods increased, and buildings associated with public utilities and with a variety of industries appeared throughout the city. A surprising number of these buildings survive, albeit now in commercial or domestic use, and they serve as reminders of the development of Oxford during a period of great economic, social, and technological change.

By no means all of Oxford's industries are explored in these three walks: building, brickmaking, quarrying, printing, papermaking, and steam engine manufacture also flourished. The seeds of Oxford's most famous industry, that of car-making, were sown in 1912 when William Morris assembled the first Bullnose Morris at his garage on Longwall Street (the facade of that building survives and there is a display about Morris in the window). After the First World War, car manufacture developed rapidly at Cowley, turning Oxford, at last, into a major industrial centre.

The walks are linear, though instructions are given for returning to the starting points. Generally the walks themselves are on flat ground, in the city centre, or along the river and canal towpaths. There are a number of flights of steps in the return routes.

Numbers in square brackets in the text refer to the numbers on the maps.

Liz Woolley
Oxford
March 2012

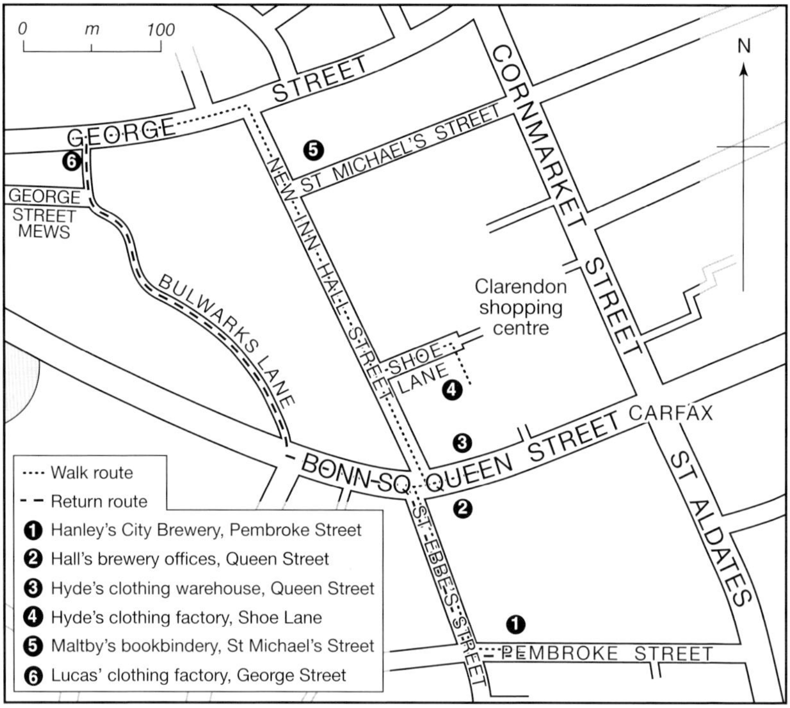

Walk 1: The City Centre

Walk 1: The City Centre (about 0.6 miles, 1 km)

Begin at the western end of Pembroke Street, near the junction with St. Ebbe's Street. The building which now houses Modern Art Oxford was erected in 1888 as a new square room and stores for **Hanley's City Brewery [1]**. Here fermentation was carried out in 'squares'—open-topped fermentation vessels in stone or slate, bolted together with the joints sealed with cement. Hanley's was founded in the early nineteenth century and occupied a large area stretching north to Queen Street. Four wells on site supplied the water used in the brewing process and there was a substantial brewhouse, offices, and several other buildings around

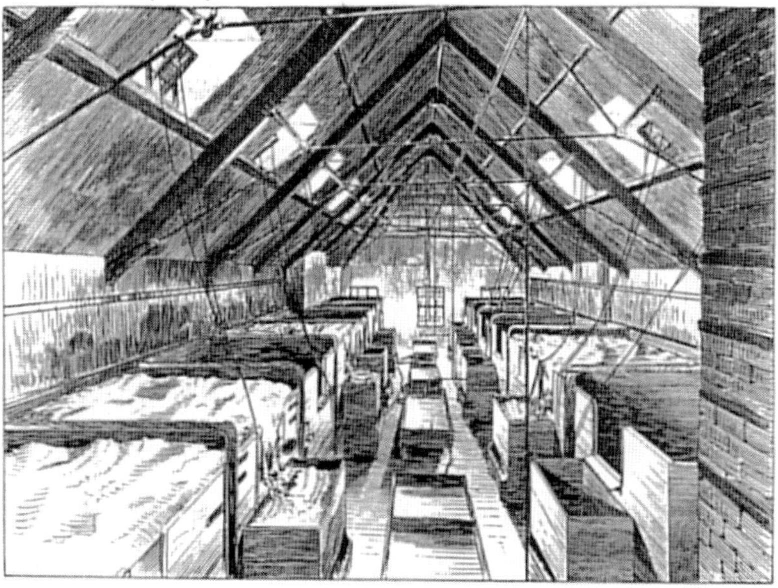

NEW FERMENTING ROOM.

The top floor of Hanley's square room and stores as illustrated in Alfred Barnard's *The Noted Breweries of Great Britain and Ireland*, vol. 3 (1891), p. 449.

a central yard. Most were erected in the later nineteenth century as the brewery, like many others, adopted new technology and expanded production to meet an ever-increasing demand for beer.

The architect of the square room was H. G. W. Drinkwater who, despite his inappropriate name, carried out a number of commissions for breweries in Oxford in the late nineteenth and early twentieth centuries. He was one of a new breed of architects who began to specialize in breweries and other similar commissions, as industrial buildings developed from being simply utilitarian sheds to being worthy of an architect's attention.

Inside the building, iron pillars marked 'Lucy and Co.' (*see Walk 2*) run through all three storeys and a plaque in the basement corridor commemorates the conversion into the Museum of Modern Art in 1966. On the top floor you can see the rooms where the 'squares' were housed.

Walk north along St. Ebbe's Street, passing on your right the large entranceway into Modern Art Oxford which led originally into the brewery yard. At the junction with Queen Street turn right; the second building along (British Home Stores) retains the facade of the **brewery offices [2]** (1914, architects Wilkins & Jeeves). Like most breweries in

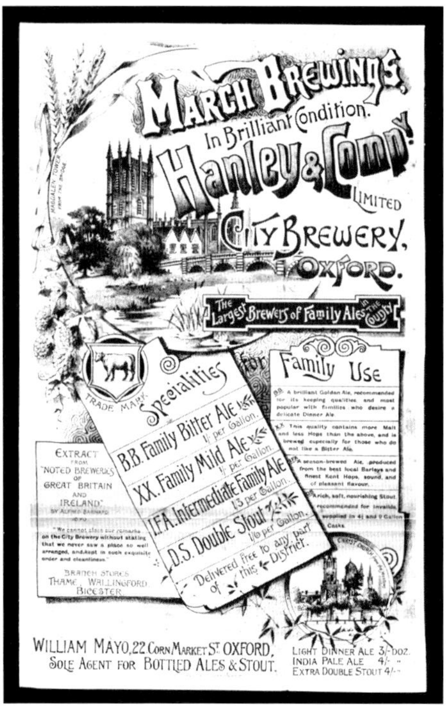

An advertisement for Hanley's ales; their Double Stout was 'recommended for invalids' and 'supplied in 4½ and 9 gallon casks'. By permission of the Bodleian Libraries, the University of Oxford. Ref: John Johnson Collection: Oxford Trade 2 (73).

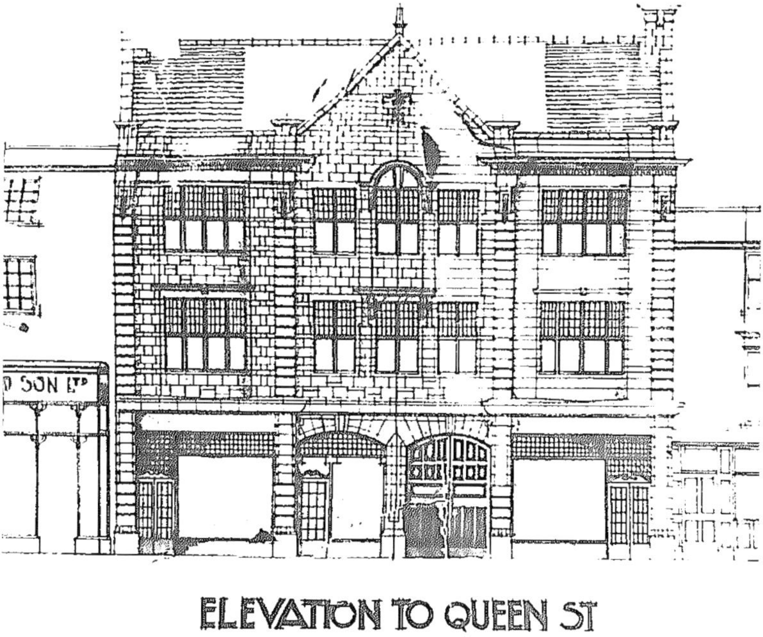

Part of Wilkins & Jeeves's plans for Hall's City Brewery offices, Queen Street, 1914. By kind permission of Oxford City Council. Ref: CEDBP 2305 (NS) 01-07-1914.

Oxford, Hanley's had by this time been taken over by Hall's, which became the main rival to Morrell's (*see Walk 2*). The elegant office frontage was no doubt intended as an advertisement for the brewery's growing business and as a contribution to the general 'improvement' of the city centre. The commercial potential of the building was maximized by incorporating three shops on the ground floor, with large curving plate-glass windows, now sadly lost.

Hyde's clothing warehouse [3] (1877) is the building with three rows of curved-headed windows on the opposite (northern) side of Queen Street. Thomas Hyde & Co. was established in 1839 and had a clothes dealership at 32 Queen Street from at least 1842. Ready-made clothes were becoming increasingly popular and Hyde's was an extensive business, with other operations in Banbury and in Abingdon. This striking new warehouse on a main commercial street in Oxford, erected at a cost of £8,500 and with a facade of Bath (rather than local) stone, served to advertise the company's products and its growing commercial success. Many contemporary warehouses and factories were being built in a similar *palazzo* style: Italianate architecture was strongly associated with commerce and the ideals of free trade, contrasting with the Gothic which dominated national architectural fashions in this period. The architect was Frederick Codd, designer of a number of elegant villas in the rapidly expanding suburb of North Oxford, and the builders were Symm & Co., founded in 1815.

Until the 1960s Hyde's warehouse had a balcony at first floor level and another on the third floor, reached by glazed doors at either end of the rows of windows. Walk a little way east along Queen Street and then look back to see an advertisement for Frank East—whose drapery store was at Carfax—high up on the side wall of the building immediately to the left of Hyde's.

Retrace your steps and turn right into New Inn Hall Street with Bonn Square on your left; shortly afterwards turn right into Shoe Lane, then right again into a dead end just before the entrance to the shopping centre. On the right-hand side of the yard is **Hyde's clothing factory [4]** (1869, architect Frederick Codd), whose functional red-brick facade is in stark contrast to the company's elegant warehouse which we have just seen on Queen Street.

Victorian industrial development brought more diverse and complex manufacturing processes, and the growing need to arrange them, and the machines that powered them, in an efficient, cost-effective, and safe manner. Here, the basement contained rooms for an engine boiler, warehouse, and sorting; on the ground floor was a steam-driven cutting room; over this was a stock room; and above, two storeys for sewing machines. Hyde's and Lucas's (another clothing firm whose building we shall see later), were the biggest employers in Oxford at this time other than the university. Between them they had several hundred workers, mainly women, some of whom worked in these factories but many of whom sewed and finished garments at home and were paid very low piece rates. A report in *Jackson's Oxford Journal* of January 1868 gives a sobering insight into their everyday lives: a woman outworker almost drowned walking from Eynsham to Oxford to deliver finished clothes to Hyde's: 'Carrying a child in her arms and a great weight of ready-made clothes on her back, she fell into a ditch six feet deep opposite the end of Binsey Lane in the dark.'

Return along Shoe Lane (the name is a corruption of a family name 'Sewys'), turn right into New Inn Hall Street and right again into St. Michael's Street. The third building on the left was, until 2010, the premises of **Maltby's bookbindery [5]**. The company was first established in 1834 in St. Helen's passage off New College Lane, near the Turf Tavern. It moved to St. Michael's Street in 1883 to occupy this early nineteenth-century shop with a characteristically large-windowed workshop above.

Thanks to the presence of the university, Oxford supported a huge number of bookbinders, far more than any other town of similar size except perhaps Cambridge. The bookbinding trade, and others of interest to the university, were controlled via a system of 'privileged persons', which meant that to enter those trades one had to matriculate and become a member of the university. The system ran in parallel with that of the city's freemen, until the Municipal Corporations Act of 1835 swept away trade restrictions.

Walk back along St. Michael's Street, turn right into New Inn Hall Street and then left into George Street. Eighty yards (75 m) along, on the western corner of Bulwarks Lane, is the former **factory of W. F. Lucas, manufacturers and ladies' outfitters [6]** (1890). The building, of plain red brick and in functional style, could accommodate 300 workers and, with its basement dining room, internal lavatories, and lifts to all floors, was designed to 'contain every modern requirement for the comfort of the employees'. Towards the end of the nineteenth century there was growing recognition of the importance of healthy and safe conditions for workers—ventilation, light, and freedom from dirt and dust, as well as restrooms, canteens, and social facilities—and newspaper reports of new buildings frequently mentioned their compliance with relevant new legislation. Like Hyde's, Lucas's was a major employer in Oxford, and local workers appear in the census from 1891 onwards, their occupation often described as 'machinist, ladies underwear factory'.

The architect of Lucas's factory was H. G. W. Drinkwater, who we met at Hanley's City Brewery, and the builder was T. H. Kingerlee whose business had been established in 1868 and had developed rapidly to become the largest building firm in Victorian and Edwardian Oxford. Kingerlee was responsible for much of the urban expansion of the city, particularly in West Oxford where Helen and Henry Roads were named after two of the founder's children. At the time of writing, Kingerlee is still a major local building company, with three of his great-great-grandsons on the management team.

This is the end of this walk. To return to the starting point, walk along Bulwarks Lane, bearing left to follow the narrow winding pathway between high walls along the course of what was the Castle ditch. Walk down a flight of steps to emerge on to New Road. Turn left into Bonn Square, walk on into Queen Street, and then turn right into St. Ebbe's Street; Modern Art Oxford is on your left.

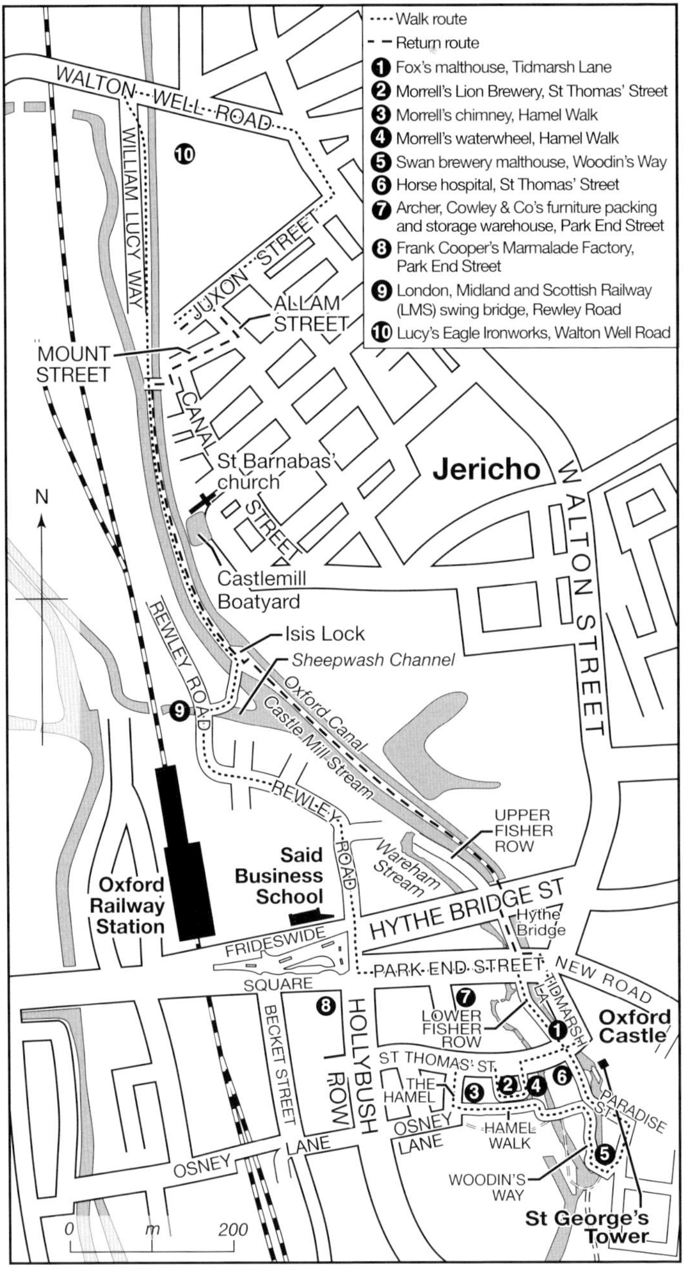

Walk 2: St. Thomas's and Jericho

Walk 2: St. Thomas's and Jericho (about 1.6 miles, 2.6 km)

Begin at the junction of New Road and Tidmarsh Lane. You are in the ancient parish of St. Thomas—traditionally the centre of Oxford's brewing industry—which by the late nineteenth century was home to four large commercial breweries and several malthouses. Walk along Tidmarsh Lane, with **Fox's malthouse [1]** on your right, a late eighteenth-century building which now houses the University Estates Directorate. Notice the closely set rows of windows on the first and second floors, indicating that the storeys within were very shallow. This is typical: the process of malting does not involve any machinery, and so only the height in which a man could comfortably work, shovelling and turning the grain, was needed. Malting requires plenty of ventilation but little light, hence these windows would originally have been shuttered rather than glazed. Moreover, a large floor area on which to spread the grain is needed, which is why malthouses often had large footprints, like this one.

Continue around the corner into St. Thomas's Street and cross the castle mill stream by Quaking Bridge. From the eleventh century until 1931 a mill stood at the foot of St. George's tower to your left. Notice behind you to the right, the back of Fox's malthouse, and ahead at 1 Fisher Row the handsome brick house built in 1790 for Edward Tawney. He owned Fox's malthouse at the time and his was one of the great brewing families to emerge in Oxford in the eighteenth century—the Tawneys, the Halls, the Treachers, and the Morrells, all related by marriage. Brewing was big business in the city and, as this imposing house suggests, brewers were men of wealth and influence. Tawney also built the almshouses next door, as recorded on the building's pediment.

Continue along St. Thomas's Street; on the left is the impressive gateway of what was, until 2002, **Morrell's Lion Brewery [2]**, now converted into housing. This is a very old brewing site: a 'Brewhouse and Garden' were mentioned in a lease of 1597, and Edward Tawney had his brewery here in the late eighteenth century. This he sold to father and son Mark and James Morrell in 1797.

The stone building at the centre of the courtyard was the head brewer's accommodation dating from Edward Tawney's time. The red brick buildings, several of whose facades have been retained in the housing development, were erected by Morrell's architect, the inappropriately named H. G. W. Drinkwater. The building to left of the entrance was the brewhouse (1879) and to the right were the offices (1892). These were just two of a clutch of new buildings designed by Drinkwater in the later nineteenth and early twentieth centuries: like many Oxford breweries, Morrell's underwent extensive expansion and upgrading in response to a growing demand for beer. Brewing was becoming more mechanized and more technologically advanced, and to remain competitive commercial breweries had to be increasingly efficient and organized; specialized buildings multiplied accordingly. As mentioned in Walk 1, Drinkwater himself was one of a new breed of architects who emerged in the later nineteenth century, and who began to specialize in brewery and other similar commissions, as industrial buildings developed from being simply utilitarian sheds to being worthy of an architect's attention.

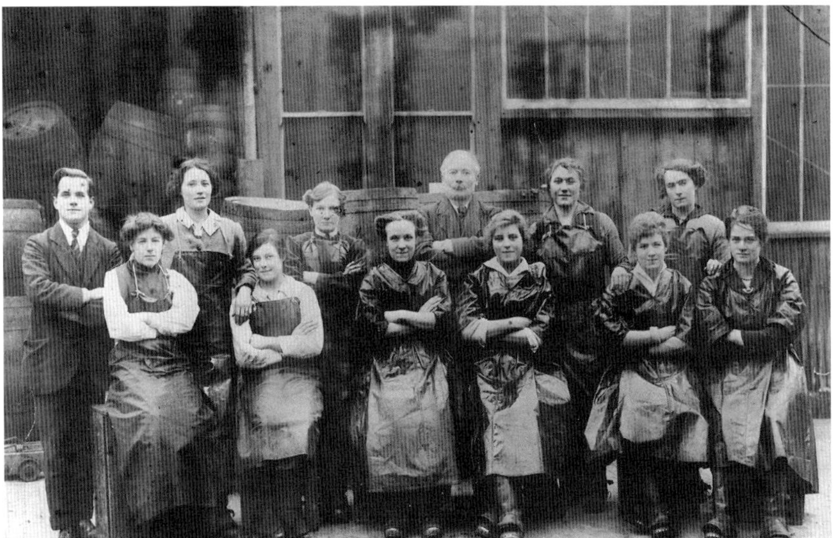

Morrell's employees in 1916, when, owing to the First World War, the company was obliged to employ women for the first time. Notice their heavy leather aprons, leather gaiters on their legs, and wooden-soled clogs. Women worked mainly in the bottling shed. John Mundy, who worked in the office, is on the far left, aged 17. He went to fight in France in 1917, but survived and returned to work at Morrell's for the rest of his career, rising to become Company Secretary. Photograph by kind permission of Mrs. Stella van Gucci.

Walk through the gates and clockwise around the courtyard to view the brewery buildings, emerging again on to St. Thomas' Street. Turn left and almost immediately left again through a narrow gap into The Hamel. At the end of this short street turn left again through a covered passage-way into Hamel Walk; on your left is the **Morrell's chimney [3]** (1901, architect H. G. W. Drinkwater) which was built when the brewery switched from water power to coal-fired boilers. A little further on, pause on the footbridge over the Wareham Stream and look to the left to see the **waterwheel [4]** which originally powered the brewery.

Continue, and just before reaching Paradise Street, turn right into Woodin's Way with the castle mill stream on your left. You are now on the Swan's Nest Island, the site of the Swan Brewery, which was first recorded in 1718. The brewery was in the hands of Sir John Treacher by 1780, and William Hall purchased it in 1795. Hall's prospered greatly, and eventually took over all the other breweries in Oxford apart from Morrell's. To the left, on the far bank of the stream, is a **malthouse [5]** (*c.* 1830), the only remnant of the Swan Brewery, the rest of whose buildings were demolished in the 1960s to make way for a British Telecom building and, later, housing. A footbridge at the tip of the island takes you back on to the 'mainland'; notice as you cross it that the malthouse's ground plan is not a rectangle.

Walk on with the malthouse on your left, through a small car park, and then left on to Paradise Street. The low red-brick building at the junction with St. Thomas' Street was the **horse hospital [6]** (1887, architect H. G. W. Drinkwater). All the local breweries used horse-drawn drays to carry their barrels, and other nearby businesses, such as Archer, Cowley & Co., the removals firm (whose building we shall see shortly), also used horse transport. Horses came here to have minor ailments seen to and to be shod—walk a little further on and look back to see the tall chimney which served the blacksmith's furnace. Most breweries had their own stables: a surviving example can be seen behind the former Elm Tree pub (site of the former Elm Tree Brewery) at the corner of Jeune Street and Cowley Road in East Oxford.

Continue ahead into (Lower) Fisher Row. Until the middle of the twentieth century this was lined with small terraced cottages, occupied mainly by families who, since medieval times, had made their living from Oxford's waterways, as river bargemen, as fishermen or, later, as canal boatmen. Walk up a flight of steps to emerge on to Park End Street. This was named after the Park End Colliery in the Forest of Dean, whose coal wharf was here (later it was the site of Philip's Tower Brewery, founded 1885). The main wharf and basin of the Oxford Canal (opened to Oxford from the Midlands in 1790) were just to the north-east under what are now the Worcester Street car park and Nuffield College, respectively.

Cross Park End Street, turn left, and walk a little way along to get a good view of the former **Archer, Cowley & Co.'s furniture packing and storage warehouse [7]** (1901) on the southern side of the street (later the 'Cantay Depositories', as it still says on the front of the building).

Warehouses were the link between industry and commerce, and towards the end of the nineteenth century they were increasingly ornate in order to impress potential customers. Archer, Cowley & Co. stored, packed, and transported furniture. Their warehouse was designed in imposing style, by the County Surveyor H. J. Tollit, no doubt to further the company's reputation as prime shippers to the administrators of the British Empire. Tollit made use of the most up-to-date building techniques: a steel frame, with floor and stairs of reinforced concrete, all the steelwork encased in concrete or brickwork. There were 3,840 square feet (357 m^2) for storage of furniture and other goods and openings between different parts of the building were protected by armoured fireproof doors which closed automatically in the event of fire. Shops on the ground floor attracted attention and provided a rental income. Walk along to the western end to see the former office, whose external woodwork is in Burmese teak, and which has, as was typical, a mosaic-tiled floor at the entrance and, around the corner, an engraved glass window with the company name. The builder was John Wooldridge, whose firm (at the time of writing) is still flourishing under the management of the fifth generation of the family.

Continue west along Park End Street, passing on your left the former site of the Eagle Steam Brewery (founded 1839, demolished 1970s). On the far corner of the junction with Hollybush Row stands **Frank Cooper's Marmalade Factory [8]** (1902), the only one of Oxford's formerly industrial buildings to be listed.

Frank Cooper had been making and selling marmalade from his shop at 84 High Street since 1874, but increased demand, and the Factories and Workshops Act of 1901—which laid down stringent rules about the kinds of conditions in which factory hands could work—may have prompted his move to this new, purpose-built, and more hygienic building with rest facilities for employees. The factory could accommodate 60 workers; their dining room and restrooms, plus two storage rooms, were on the top floor. On the second floor women cut up fruit in a long, well-lit room with large curve-headed windows. Bottling and packing (or 'tying down') took place on the floor below and the cooking of fruit was done beyond the yard on the ground floor, in a boiling room equipped with copper (later stainless

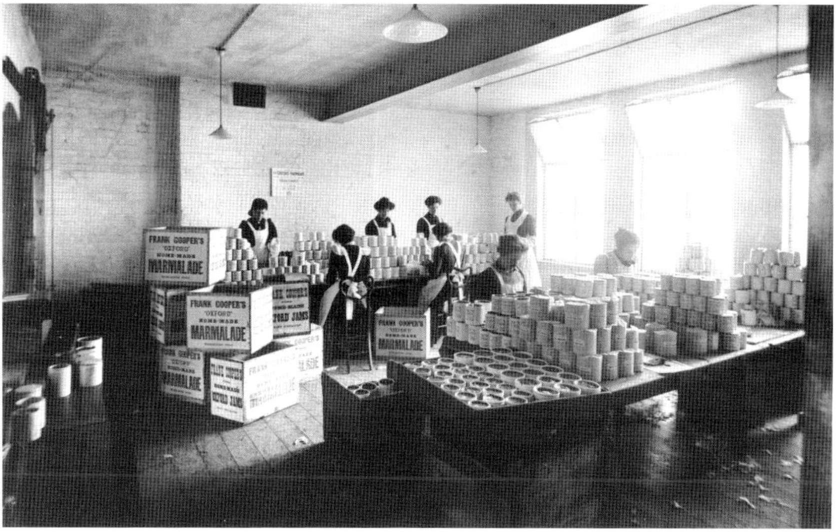

The packing or 'tying-down' room on the first floor of Frank Cooper's Marmalade Factory, *c.* 1905. © Oxfordshire County Council, Oxfordshire History Centre. Ref: D260039a.

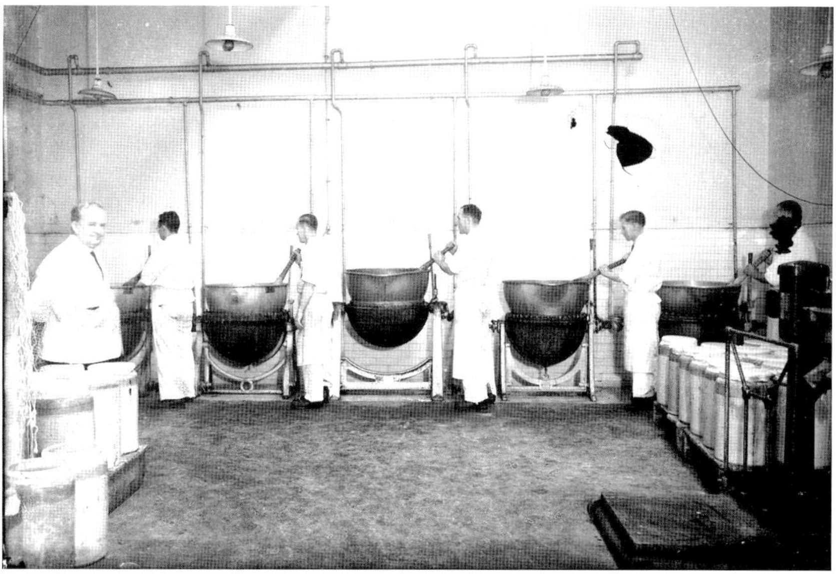

Stirring vats of marmalade in the boiling room, *c.* 1937. © Oxfordshire County Council, Oxfordshire History Centre. Ref: D261714a.

steel) vats heated through steam jackets by a boiler in the adjacent boiler-house with its large chimney. The yard, the boiling room, the boiler-house, and the chimney, as well as further storerooms added when the factory expanded production after the First World War, can be seen by going in through the entrance on Hollybush Row. The curved office extension on the corner was added in 1925.

Frank Cooper was a vigorous promoter of his products, emphasizing the home-made purity and health-giving properties of his marmalade, as well as its upper-class appeal. Soon after opening his new factory, he commissioned the well-known Oxford photographer Henry Taunt to produce a city guidebook: the chapter entitled 'Gastronomical Oxford' briefly mentions Oxford sausages before eulogizing for page after page Cooper's marmalade and this wonderful new building 'fitted with the best modern improvements, and everything is done that is possible to obtain the highest standard of quality, purity and wholesomeness'. Cooper was proud to obtain royal patronage for his 'Oxford' marmalade and the British Medical Association conference of 1936 was told that 'The "Oxford" has played a leading part in the life of the Varsity for many years... It is even hinted—admittedly upon somewhat doubtful authority—that a certain quantity must be consumed before one can secure a degree.'

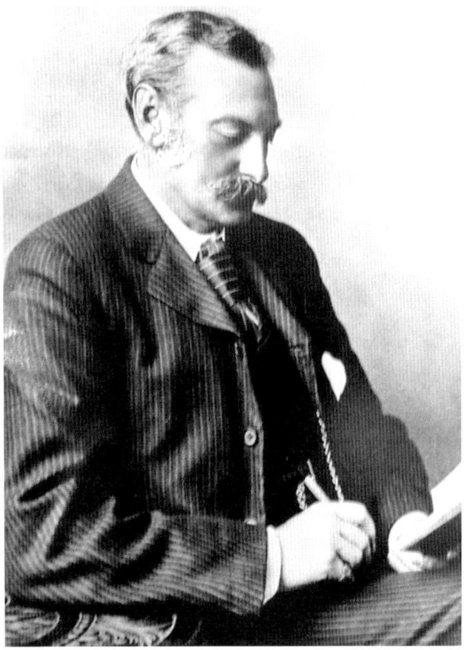

Frank Cooper, 1844–1927.
© Oxfordshire County Council, Oxfordshire History Centre.
Ref: B3/AD/P&/1.

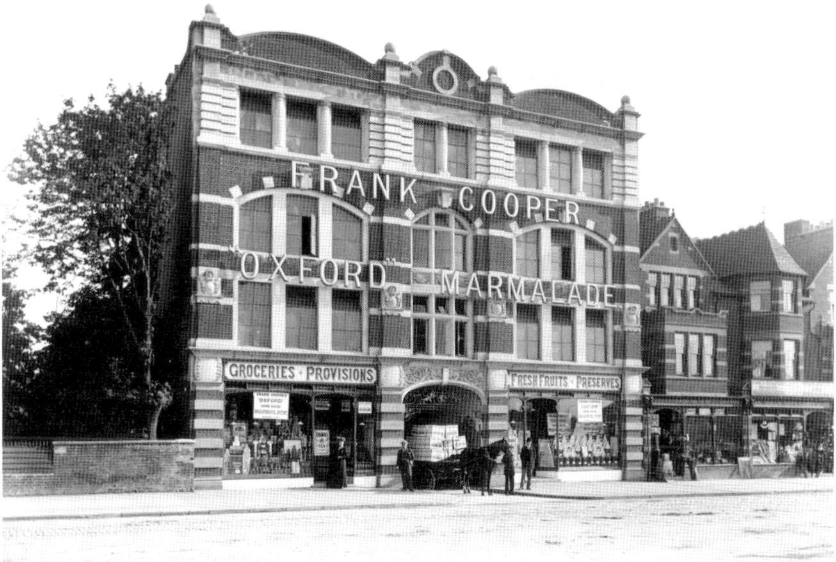

The front of the factory soon after opening, *c.* 1904. A horse and cart, loaded with boxes of marmalade, stand in the central entranceway. Notice the two shops either side; these were replaced with offices, with much smaller windows, within a couple of years. © Oxfordshire County Council, Oxfordshire History Centre. Ref: D210145a.

The factory was in a prime position opposite the then two railway stations, and its elaborate facade declares Cooper's confidence as a businessman: he even had oranges carved into the stonework. Some people say that the balls on the roofline are oranges. The architect was Herbert Quinton, a disciple of the Arts and Crafts movement and designer of some of the more notable houses in North Oxford. The builder was T. H. Kingerlee whose business had been established in 1868 and had developed rapidly to become the largest building firm in Victorian and Edwardian Oxford. As mentioned in Walk 1, Kingerlee were responsible for much of the urban expansion of the city, particularly in West Oxford where Helen and Henry Roads were named after two of the founder's children. At the time of writing, Kingerlee is still a major local building company, with three of his great-great-grandsons on the management team.

Cross Frideswide Square and walk along Rewley Road with the Said Business School on your left. The road takes you around the back of the School, through a housing estate, and over a small bridge. To the left is the

London, Midland and Scottish Railway (LMS) swing bridge [9] (1850–1, constructed to designs by Robert Stephenson), one of only two swing bridges in England which are scheduled monuments. It connected the station of the London and North Western Railway (LNWR, later LMS), which stood where the Said Business School is now, with the locomotive depot and lines to Bicester and Bletchley to its north.

The swing bridge carried the track across the Sheepwash channel (a navigation cut connecting the River Thames with the canal), and swivelled horizontally to allow boats through. In 1853, a railway engine toppled into the water, the driver having failed to realize that the bridge had been opened to allow a boat to pass. Two men could open and close the swing bridge in less than five minutes using a hand-operated winding mechanism, the teethed gearwheels of which can be seen on two posts either side of the bridge, about half way along its length (the best view is from the path which leads west under the modern railway bridge).

In 1890, and again in 1906, the upper parts of the bridge were reconstructed using an early type of steel girder, probably to take heavier locomotives. Like the LMS station, the swing bridge closed to passenger traffic in 1951, though it remained in operation until the nearby goods yard closed in 1984. At the time of writing (2012) it is awaiting restoration by the Oxford Preservation Trust, English Heritage, its owners Network Rail, and other partners.

With the swing bridge behind you and the Sheepwash channel on your right, cross Rewley Road and walk ahead along a path and over a footbridge. Turn left on to the towpath, with the canal on your right and the castle mill stream on your left, and head north. The canal, designed by James Brindley, the pioneering canal engineer, and his assistant Samuel Simcock, provided a link with the Midlands coal fields. Until then coal had to be shipped at great expense down the east coast from Newcastle, through the Port of London, and up the Thames. The arrival of cheap Midlands coal in 1790 had a considerable impact on the local economy, and played a major role in the development of industry in Oxford, bringing fuel and raw materials to industrial sites and providing the means to transport finished goods and waste products away. The coming of the railway to Oxford in 1844 eventually put an end to business on the canal (having killed off the city's once great coaching trade within only a decade).

About 320 yards (300 m) along, on the opposite bank of the canal, is the site of the Jericho or Castlemill boatyard which sits at the foot of St. Barnabas's church (1869). This was originally a coal wharf, and was later used as a yard for hire and repair of canal boats. The boatyard's closure in 2007 prompted a vigorous and ultimately successful campaign to prevent the site being sold purely for commercial housing and at the time of writing (2012) it is awaiting mixed-use redevelopment by community groups.

After about another 600 yards (500 m) there is a large five-storey red brick development of flats on the far bank of the canal. These were built in 2006 on the site of **Lucy's Eagle Ironworks [10]**, which was founded in 1812 by William Carter and moved here in 1825. In the late nineteenth century this was one of several Oxford iron foundries, including Taylor's of St. Ebbe's and Dean & Son of East Oxford.

Initially Lucy's catered for the local market, making agricultural machinery and cast iron for ornamental ironwork and lamp-posts—their name can been seen on railings and lamp posts all around Oxford, and on pillars in Hanley's City Brewery square room (*see Walk 1*). In 1897 Lucy's expanded their product range to include shelving and storage equipment which were sold nationwide; they built the rolling-stack system of library shelving used underground in the Bodleian, among many other university and public libraries. Over the next ten years Lucy's buildings multiplied and diversified to include new offices, storerooms, a

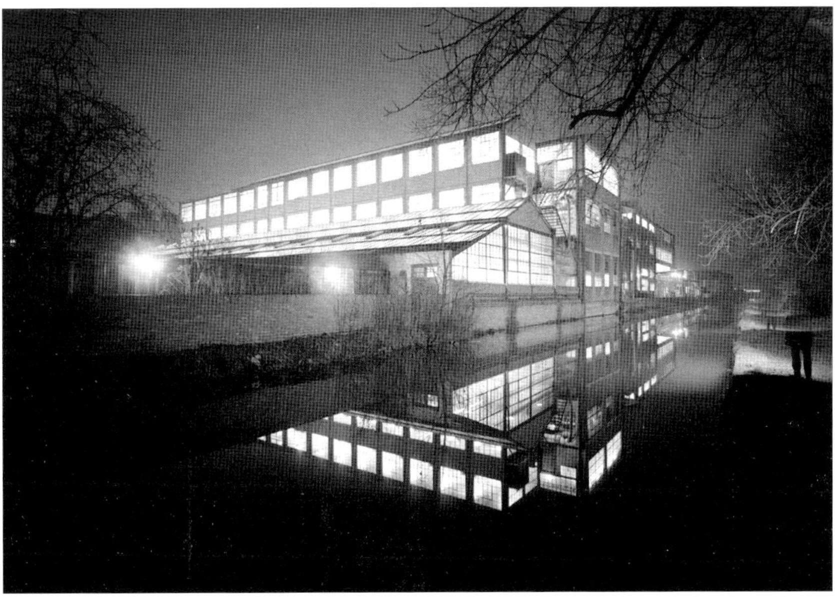

Lucy's Eagle Ironworks at night, with the canal in the foreground, 1964.
© Oxfordshire County Council, Oxfordshire History Centre. Ref: D271597a.

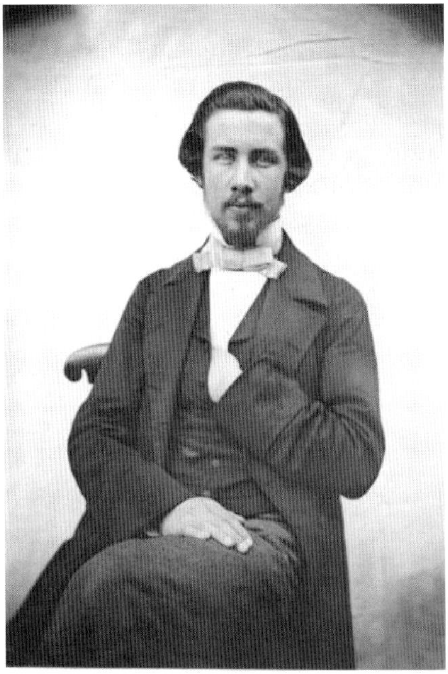

William Lucy (d. 1873) took over the Eagle Iron Foundry in the early 1860s and it bore his name until closure in 2005. By kind permission of W. Lucy & Co. Ltd.

workshop and fitting-shop, and additions to the foundry itself. By the early twentieth century the works occupied an extensive site and were a major employer in Jericho. In 2003 Philip Pullman portrayed the Eagle Ironworks in his novel *Lyra's Oxford.*

Just before bridge 242, take a sloping path to the left up on to Walton Well Road. Turn right to go over the bridge, noticing first 'William Lucy Way' to the left. Near the end of Walton Well Road on the right is the Arts and Crafts inspired offices (1905, architect George Gardiner), the only Lucy's building to escape demolition after the foundry closed in 2005. Attached to the eastern end of the office building is a handsome factory clock, and nearby a set of iron gates and two stone eagles. Turn right into Walton Street and right again into Juxon Street, at the end of which two more eagle-topped gateways remain.

This is the end of this walk. To return to the starting point, walk from Juxon Street into Allam Street and turn right into Mount Street. Here a bridge takes you over the canal. Walk south along the towpath, with the canal on your left and the mill stream on your right. The wharves of the Canal Company, used for coal, stone, and timber, spread along the opposite bank from here all the way to bridge 243. Walk over this bridge and continue along the towpath. Cross over Hythe Bridge Street (*hythe* is a Saxon word meaning 'wharf' or 'landing place') and down a flight of steps on the other side, along Middle Fisher Row. Like Lower Fisher Row this was, until the middle of the twentieth century, lined with small terraced cottages, occupied mainly by families who, since medieval times, had made their living from Oxford's waterways. In the nineteenth century the Beesleys ran an osier works here, where willow rods were stripped and woven into baskets and fish- and eel-traps. Climb another flight of steps to reach Park End Street; turn left and Tidmarsh Lane is shortly on your right.

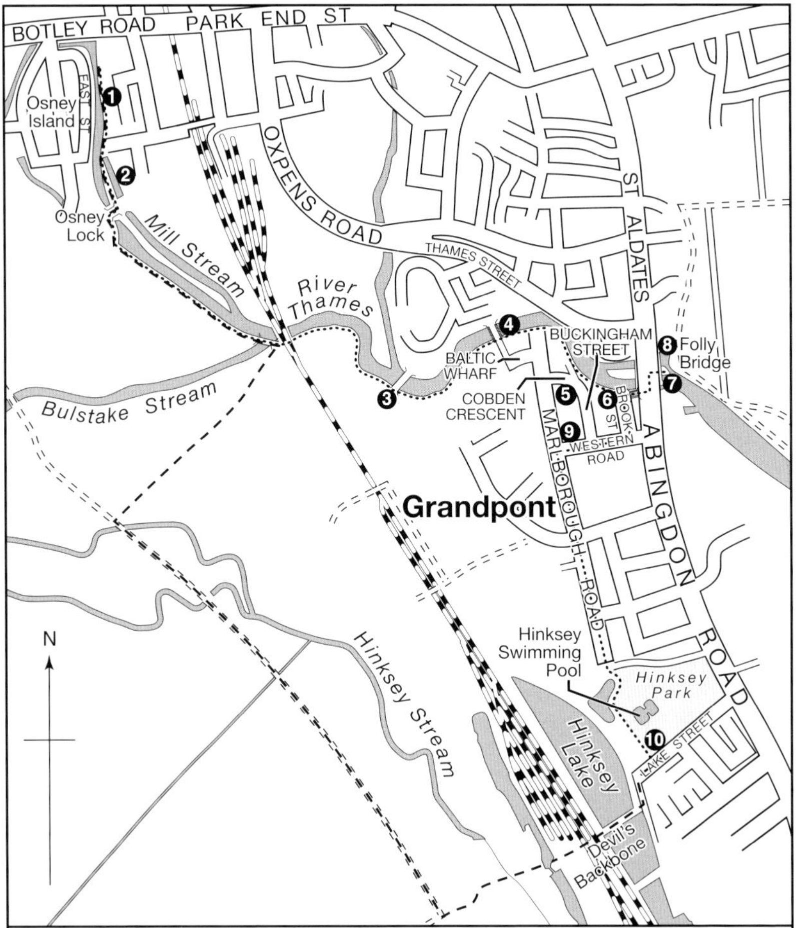

1. Electric Lighting Station, Canon Wharf, Osney
2. Osney Mill, Osney Lock
3. Gasworks railway bridge
4. Gasworks pipe bridge, Baltic Wharf
5. Site of North's mineral water factory, Cobden Crescent
6. Salter's boat-building workshop, Brook Street
7. Salter's offices, club room and waiting rooms, Folly Island
8. Salter's warehouse and workshop, Folly Bridge
9. Site of first (Grandpont) railway station, Marlborough Road
10. Waterworks pumping station, Lake Street

····· Walk route

– – Return route

0 m 400

Walk 3: Osney and South Oxford

Walk 3: Osney and South Oxford (about 2 miles, 3.2 km)

Begin at the corner of North and East Streets on Osney Island, off the Botley Road. Walk along East Street with the river on your left until you see the large and imposing red and yellow brick building of the **Electric Lighting Station [1]** (1892, architect A. P. Brevitt) across the water.

In many places electricity was first generated on private estates and in Oxford a few private generators were in use in the 1880s, including one at the Oxford Union on St. Michael's Street. In 1882 the Electric Lighting Act opened the way to public generation of electricity but it was not until June 1892 that the works of the Oxford Electric Company Ltd. opened, consisting of this generating station at Canon Wharf in Osney, a central switching station in Broad Street, and two small substations at King (now Merton) Street and Carfax. The generating station used steam-driven turbines, fuelled by coal, and pioneered an innovative system for transporting electricity across the network which became known as the 'Oxford System'.

The opening of the plant was hailed by Hilaire Belloc in his unsuccessful entry for the Newdigate Prize for poetry in 1893, on 'The Benefits of the Electric Light'. Ladies at the opening ceremony were encouraged to declare that no house was properly furnished unless it had the electric light and *Jackson's Oxford Journal* reported that 'Long before dusk the streets in the centre of town were thronged with crowds of persons to witness the lighting of the arc lamps. It was, however, after 10 o'clock before the current was turned on, and many persons left without seeing the light, which was brilliant and steady.'

Production began on a modest scale: initially electricity was supplied to just five street lamps and eleven business premises. But in its first year the company installed 7,000 35-watt lamps and by 1895 almost all the colleges and some university buildings were electrified. The late nineteenth and early twentieth centuries saw rapid growth in the use of electricity in homes, places of entertainment, industry, and transport, and over the next ten years the generating station was expanded five times to keep up with demand.

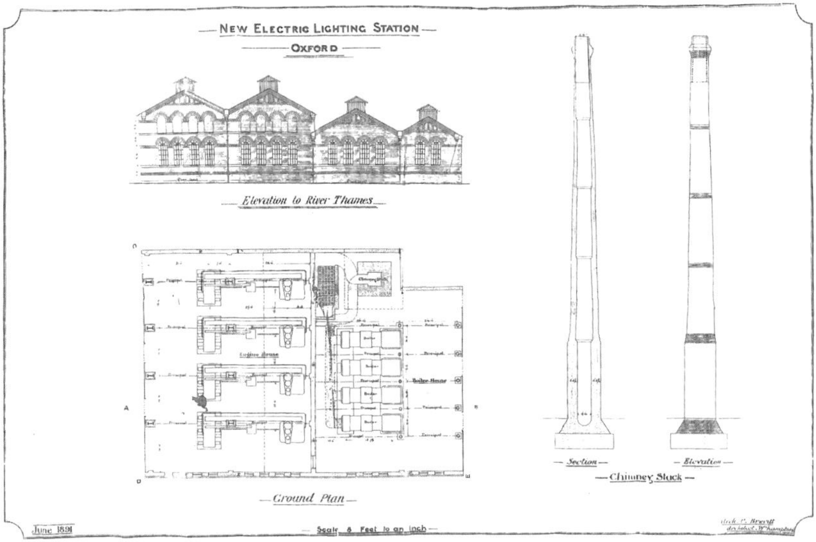

Part of A. P. Brevitt's plans for the new Electric Lighting Station at Osney, 1891. By kind permission of Oxford City Council. Ref: CEDBP 1771A (OS) 06-08-1891.

Local people cursed the smuts from the station which fell on to their washing. However, there were compensations: water which had been used to cool the turbines was pumped back into the river hot, and people could swim and wash their hair here all year round. Children also dived for pieces of coal which had fallen from barges, and which provided a welcome addition to the family grate.

The lively facade of structural polychrome brickwork was perhaps intended to act as an advertisement for the new industry and to distinguish it from the rather more utilitarian gasworks further downstream. In 1905 the architect Herbert Quinton, who had designed Frank Cooper's marmalade factory on Park End Street in 1902 (*see Walk 2*), added the small northern extension which includes an oriel window lighting the chief engineer's office. It has been said that this was so that he could keep an eye out for his employees fishing from the adjacent wharf, though it must also have allowed him to see barges delivering coal by means of a hopper which descended from a gantry over the river. The southern extension was built in the 1920s.

The electricity station was converted from coal to oil in 1963 after decades of complaints about the dirt, but it closed in 1969, when electricity began to be supplied from Didcot Power Station. The building was later used by the university as an engineering laboratory but at the time of writing (2012) is awaiting redevelopment.

Continue along the towpath to Osney Lock; on the other side of the river stands the red brick **Osney Mill [2]** (main building 1845, left-hand part late eighteenth century). A mill was built here soon after the foundation of Osney Abbey in 1129; it was one of at least fifteen watermills in the city in the medieval period, mostly corn mills. Their building caused numerous disputes over water rights and many changes in branches of the river close to the west and south sides of the city: at Osney the mill stream became the main course of the river, as it is today, when the lock was built by labour from the nearby castle prison in 1790.

By the mid thirteenth century, Osney Abbey, one of the largest and wealthiest in the country, had not only a corn mill but also a fulling mill (in which fullers' earth was pounded into newly woven cloth by hammers to scour and cleanse it), and later a gig mill (to raise the nap on cloth). After dissolution in 1542, the abbey's extensive lands and buildings, including its mills, were given to the recently refounded Oxford college of Christ Church.

There was a grist mill here in the early seventeenth century, and during the Civil War (1642–51) the mill was used to grind gunpowder. In 1775 part of Osney Mill was being used as a china factory, and by 1829 the tenant had built saw mills; two bone mills (to grind bones for agricultural fertilizer) were added in the 1840s when the mill was rebuilt in its present form. By 1876 it had become a flour mill and it was enlarged in the later nineteenth century so that it could be driven by steam rollers.

In 1898 the mill was taken over by W. H. Munsey who milled flour mainly for bread-making. By 1940 the electricity station upstream was taking so much water from the river to cool its turbines that the mill was forced to switch from waterwheel-power to electricity. This proved to be a disastrous move: in 1946 flour dust clogged the electrical circuits and the building suffered a devastating fire.

Coincidentally, mass-produced sliced bread was becoming more popular and the Munsey family decided not to rebuild a bread-flour mill at Osney but instead to take over Clark's Mill at Wantage, which milled flour only for biscuits. At the time of writing (2012) W. H. Munsey's grandson Bill and great-grandson Paul continue to run the business from there, supplying small craft-bakers. Bill Munsey lives here at Osney in the white Mill House and has developed the burnt-out mill buildings into flats, powered by hydroelectricity using an Archimedean screw set into the mill race to the side of the building.

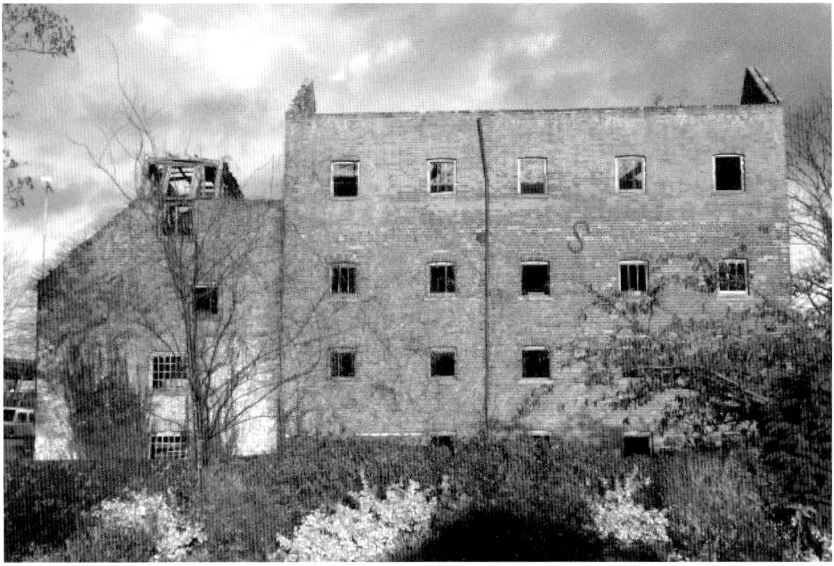

Osney Mill in 2009, having been gutted by fire and derelict for over sixty years. Work began on its restoration and conversion into housing in 2011. Photograph by the author.

Continue along the towpath, with the river on your left. After a quarter of a mile (400 m) go over a footbridge, just before passing under the railway bridge, and notice Bulstake Stream branching off to the right. This was originally the main channel of the Thames before the lock was constructed at Osney in 1790. Keep to the towpath and stop when you reach a bench from which there is a good view ahead of the **gasworks railway bridge [3]** (1886).

The gasworks was Oxford's first, large-scale, markedly 'industrial' building complex, established here in 1818 by the Oxford & District Gas Company, initially just on the north-eastern (left-hand) bank of the Thames. Gas lighting was introduced in 1819 and later the scale of gas manufacture increased significantly as it was used more and more for cooking, for space and water heating, and for powering industrial engines. The gasworks expanded accordingly and in 1882 acquired further land on the south-western bank, eventually occupying a site of nineteen acres.

In 1886 a spur of the Great Western Railway was built to bring coal to the works from the station; previously coal had been transported by cart, causing unpopular congestion on the roads. The bridge carrying the railway across the Thames, which you now see ahead of you, was designed

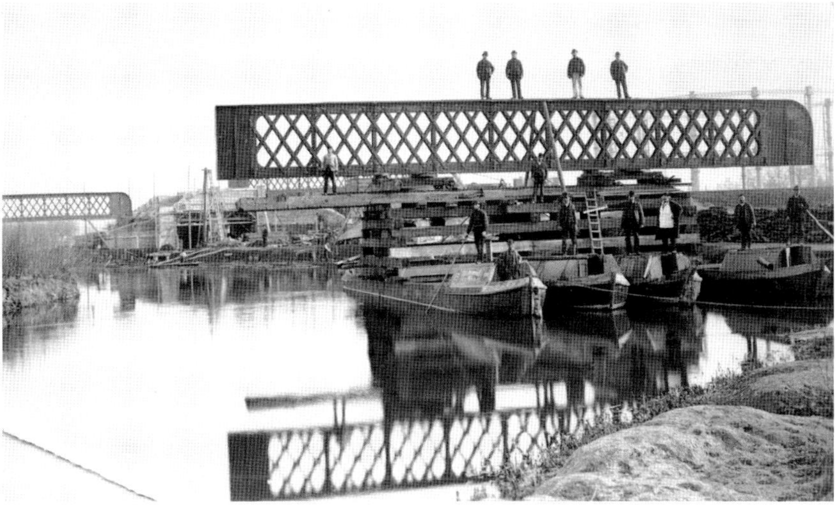

A section of the gasworks railway bridge being floated along the Thames on barges during the bridge's construction in 1886. Health and safety were obviously not major concerns. © Oxfordshire County Council, Oxfordshire History Centre. Ref: HT140.

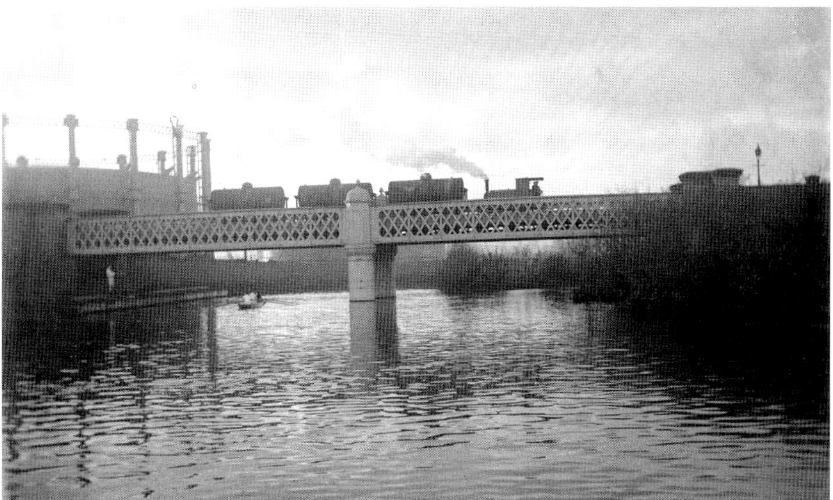

The railway bridge with a gasworks locomotive crossing it and one of the gasholders behind, 1925. © Oxfordshire County Council, Oxfordshire History Centre. Ref: D254356a.

by the nationally eminent civil engineer Thomas Hawksley and cost almost £4,000. The central cast-iron piers are sunk twenty feet (6 m) into the river bed and the end piers are built from engineering bricks, 'Staffordshire Blues', which are extremely dense, heavy, and hence strong, and which were often used in industrial buildings and structures.

The bridge was a multifunctional structure: one half was used as a cart-road, the other half supported a single track of rails, and a footway allowed workers to cross between the sites on the north and south banks of the river. On the northern side the rails were carried on an elevated wooden gantry eleven feet (3.5 m) above the ground as far as the retort house, where coal was heated to make gas. Coal arrived daily, from Yorkshire or Derbyshire, and was moved about the gasworks system by small saddle tank engines. A turntable enabled engines to return to the station, pushing the now empty wagons back along the single track.

Continue along the towpath, with what is now a nature reserve on your right, and imagine how very different this area was when the gasworks were functioning. Apparently W. H. Auden brought visitors here because, as an admirer of T. S. Eliot's poem *The Waste Land*, he thought the St. Ebbe's gasworks to be the most beautiful place on earth.

Pass under the railway bridge, glancing up to see the original cast-iron mains pipes, and continue as far as a small white footbridge across the river. This was the **gasworks pipe bridge [4]** (1927, engineers Head Wrightson & Co. Ltd., of Thornaby-on-Tees, as written on one of the metal uprights of the bridge itself). These two bridges are the last vestiges of the St. Ebbe's gasworks, which closed in 1960 and whose buildings were demolished in the late 1960s and early 1970s, as were those of many Victorian gasworks across the country. At the same time the grid of streets lined with working-class terraces, which grew up in St. Ebbe's following the arrival of the gasworks in 1818, underwent large-scale slum clearance. On the northern site there is now a small housing estate, and Gas Street, on which stood the original entrance to the works, has become Preachers Lane.

There were wharves on both sides of the river here in the nineteenth century; Basson's Baltic timber yard and wharf stood on the site beside you, now occupied by Pembroke College's Sir Geoffrey Arthur building (1987). It was a landing-place for pine from Scandinavia, in huge demand as a building material when Oxford's suburbs were undergoing rapid expansion in the Victorian period.

Continue east along the towpath, passing the junction of Buckingham Street and Cobden Crescent on your right. On this corner stood **North's mineral water works [5]**, brewers of 'Non-alcoholic Hop Bitter Beer and Stout, and Pure Home Brewed Ginger Beer and Manufacturer of

Non-Alcoholic Wines, Cordials and Fruit Syrup and Mineral Water'. The factory used all the latest steam-driven equipment, and could produce 12,000 bottles of mineral water a day. The building was demolished in 1970 and the current block of flats built to the same outline.

A little further on along the towpath a winch overhanging the path marks your arrival in the territory of **Salter's Steamers**. The company was founded in 1858 and by 1887 occupied four sites on and around Folly Bridge, including the square block-like building to the right of the winch which was until 2000 a **boatbuilding workshop [6]**. It is now a block of flats, named after the mother of the firm's current owner.

Continue over a footbridge and cross Abingdon Road at the traffic lights. Turn left on to Folly Bridge and almost immediately right, down a flight of steps between buildings to the water's edge. From here you can see another three Salter's sites: where you are standing on Folly Bridge Island, the tall narrow building with red window frames was **Salter's offices, club room, and waiting room [7]** (1900, architect Stephen Salter who was a member of the family).

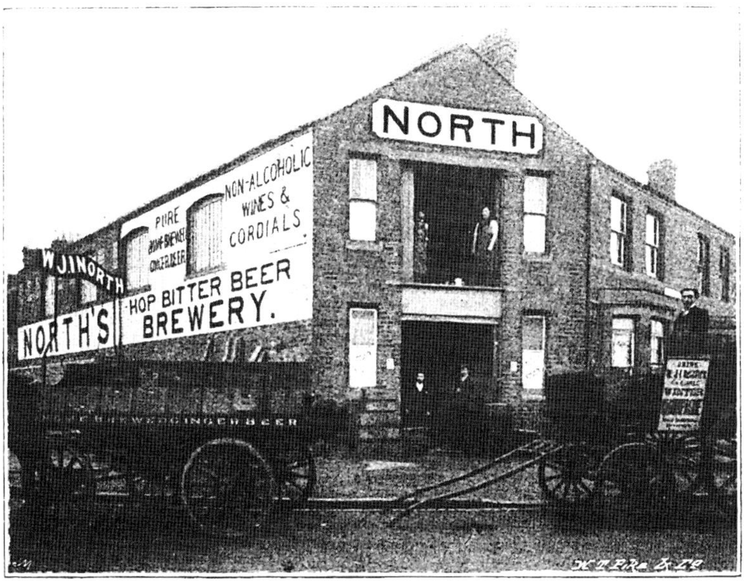

1 AND 3, COBDEN CRESCENT.

The premises of Mr. W. J. I. North, established 1896, on the corner of Buckingham Street and Cobden Crescent. From *Views and Reviews: Oxford*, W. T. Pike & Co., 1897, by kind permission of the Oxfordshire History Centre.

JACKSON'S OXFORD JOURNAL. SATURDAY

OUR ILLUSTRATIONS.

SALTER AND CO'S NEW OFFICES AT FOLLY BRIDGE.

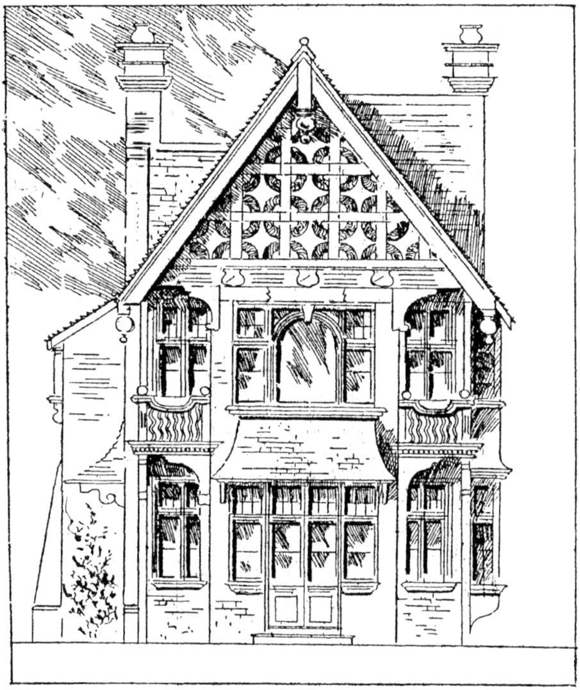

The above sketch is from the plans of Mr. Stephen Salter, F.R.I.B.A., for Messrs. Salter and Co.'s steam boat offices at the Slope, Folly Bridge.

Salter's new offices, club room, and waiting room on Folly Bridge Island illustrated in *Jackson's Oxford Journal*, 10 November 1900. The assistance of the Oxfordshire History Centre in obtaining this image is acknowledged.

The adjacent white warehouse (now Salter's main office) was built in 1835–6 by a previous boatbuilding firm, Carter, Sherratt & Hall. To the south, across the stream, was a Salter's yard and boatbuilding workshop, where Hertford College accommodation is now. To the north of Folly Bridge, the building which since 1977 has been the Head of the River pub was Salter's first **warehouse and workshop [8]**. It was built in 1827, but the adjacent wharf dates back to at least 1638. Isaac King ran a boatyard from here and brothers John and Stephen Salter, who had a boatbuilding business in Wandsworth, took it over from him when they arrived in Oxford in 1858. Notice another winch overhanging the water in what is now the pub's courtyard garden.

Salter's built all kinds of boats—rowing boats, racing craft, canoes, college barges, pleasure boats, steam launches, paddle steamers, lifeboats, and military craft—which they sold throughout Britain and abroad. By the end of the nineteenth century they had become one of the country's foremost inland boatbuilders, manufacturing up to 350 boats a year here at Folly Bridge and at their other site a mile downstream at Donnington Bridge. As business boomed the Salter family itself rose in status: it produced two mayors of Oxford, an MP for the university, and a waterman to the Queen.

Salter's played a major role in the commercialization of leisure on the Thames. They became one of the largest riverboat operators in the country, having started to run passenger boats from Oxford to Kingston in 1888. In partnership with the Great Western Railway they offered round trips whereby the downstream journey to destinations such as

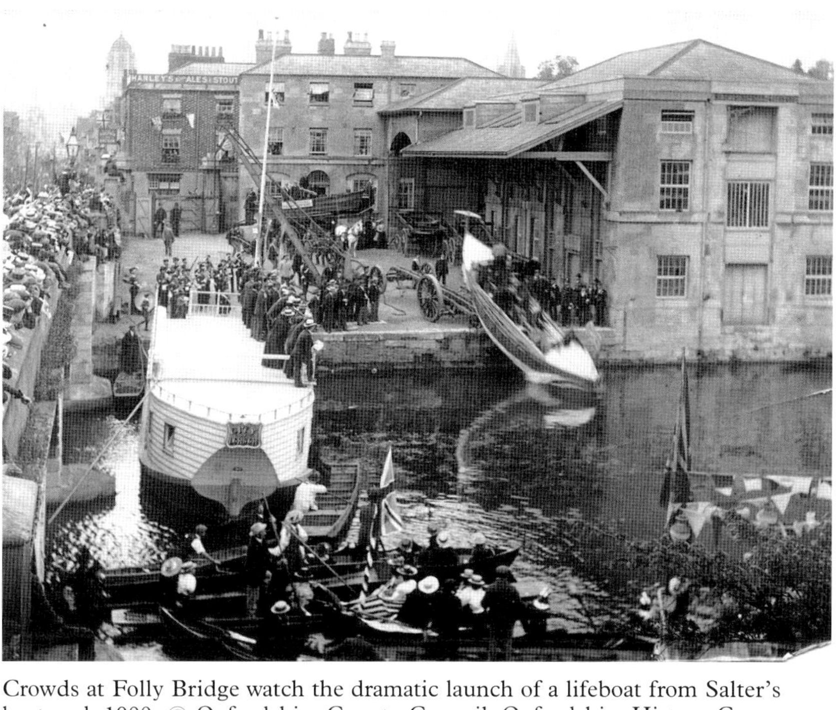

Crowds at Folly Bridge watch the dramatic launch of a lifeboat from Salter's boatyard, 1900. © Oxfordshire County Council, Oxfordshire History Centre. Ref: D254071a.

Abingdon was by boat, the return by train. They also went into private boat-hire which is now their main business.

Return to the pavement on Folly Bridge, turn left and cross back over the Abingdon Road at the traffic lights, retracing your steps across the footbridge ahead. Turn left into Brook Street; on the left a red-brick block of flats replaced a Salter's workshop, and on the right Arthur Salter Court, named after the current owner's father, was built in 2005 on the site of yet another. Beyond, four concrete terraced houses in Buckingham Street are some of the sixty or so properties which Salter's built to rent out to their workers and others. The company employed a large number of local people—the 'Salter's Navy'—some of whom were seconded to the nearby gasworks during the winter months.

Turn right into Western Road and continue to the junction with Marlborough Road. Near this corner, long before any of these houses or the former Marlborough House pub were built, was **Oxford's first (Grandpont) railway station [9]**, opened in June 1844 when the Didcot to Oxford branch of the Great Western terminated here (hence the name 'Western Road'). At the opening of the line there were gala celebrations and *Jackson's Oxford Journal* reported that large crowds watched enthralled as 'one of those rampageous, dragonnading fire-devils . . . arrived at a sufficiently astonishing rate, and though gasping for breath and shining with heat, seemed to have turned not one hair more than was deemed proper by each spectator, even after its long and whirlwind chase'.

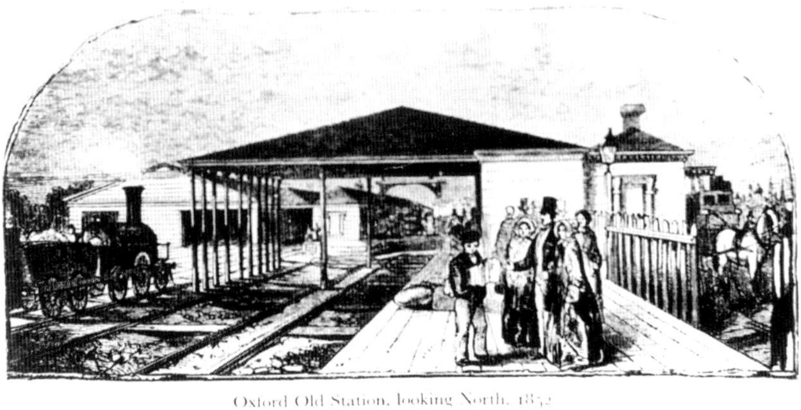

Grandpont station just before its closure in 1852, looking north towards the river. The goods shed is behind and to the left. © Oxfordshire County Council, Oxfordshire History Centre. Ref: D269243a.

The station was a mainly wooden structure with two broad-gauge tracks and small wagon turntables at the terminus ends; a further three tracks ran alongside serving a large goods shed just behind. A single track continued northwards 400 yards (365 m) to the river bank where a small jetty and crane were used to load and unload river barges carrying coal and other goods. Water for the railway engines was obtained straight from the river and stored within the station area in large barrels, which were then manhandled on to the locomotives to fill the tanks.

Grandpont station was short-lived: in 1850 the GWR extended its line north to Birmingham, and trains arriving here now had to reverse southwards to Millstream Junction before continuing on north. Grandpont station therefore became highly inconvenient and on 1 October 1852 a new GWR station was opened on the present railway station site, adjacent to the London and North Western (LNWR) one which had been built the year before (*see Walk 2*). The Grandpont terminus was closed to passengers but continued to be used as a goods station until November 1872, when broad gauge was finally abandoned in Oxford.

Continue south along Marlborough Road, which was laid out in the early 1880s along the course of the redundant railway track. Land for the line, the station site, and the approach road (now Western Road) had been raised above flood level and was therefore ideal ground for house-building; most of the houses on Marlborough Road have front rooms on a higher level (on the embankment) than the rooms at the back.

At the end of Marlborough Road cross a footbridge over Eastwyke ditch and enter Hinksey Park though a kissing gate. Walk a few yards to the right and look under the footbridge to see the supporting pillar, a remnant of the old railway line itself.

The park was originally the landscaped grounds of the Oxford waterworks, laid out in 1854 and made accessible to the public in the 1920s. When the works closed in 1934 the land was given to the city to be made into a recreational park. In 1936 the former cooling pond was converted into the boating lake on your right and the filter-beds into swimming and paddling pools further on to the left.

Continue to the far side of the park to the red brick **waterworks pumping station [10]** (1854, designed by engineer James Jones who became the works' first manager). There had been a pumping station near Folly Bridge since the seventeenth century but it depended on a waterwheel for power, unreliable when the river was flowing slowly. Moreover, the water it pumped was unfiltered and there were five sewage outfalls and the gasworks upstream. Naturally, therefore, most Oxford inhabitants preferred to rely on wells and in 1851 less than 8 per cent of houses took

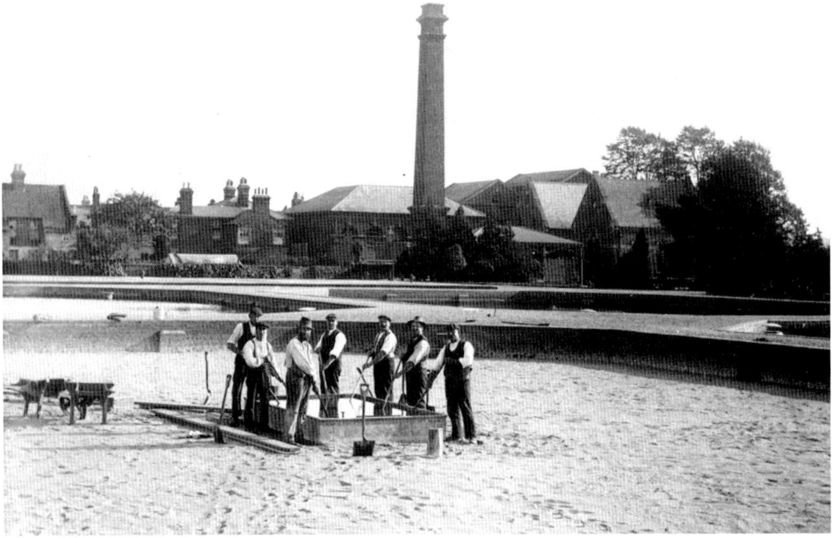

Workmen washing sand in the waterworks filter beds in 1914. The beds were installed in 1883, and now form Hinksey outdoor swimming pool. The pumping station with its chimney can be seen in the background. © Oxfordshire County Council, Oxfordshire History Centre. Ref: D263922a.

the city water supply. Devastating cholera outbreaks in the late 1840s and early 1850s focused attention on the city's poor sanitation and in 1854 the corporation bought the lake here at South Hinksey (formed by the extraction of gravel for the GWR embankment in 1850) and built this new pumping station.

Demand for clean water rose rapidly—by 1885 all the houses in the city were on the mains and the works were supplying 2 million gallons a day. At first the pumping station employed steam power, initially using beam engines and later compound vertical and horizontal engines. To house these enormous engines the buildings had to be tall; light and ventilation were also needed, and the high, round-headed windows of the original pump-house and boiler-house fronting Lake Street are typical.

In 1862 a new house for a Butterly rotative engine was built on the corner, and in 1881 a chimney (now demolished). In 1884 a house to accommodate a Davey low-lift engine was added; another was built in 1890 for a Worthington horizontal engine near the park entrance (see the plan opposite).

The design of waterworks buildings, and their landscaped settings, were used by water companies as a public expression of purity, improvement, confidence, and reliability to customers. Hence they are often rather grand—here they could be considered to be 'classical', perhaps evoking Roman baths. The buildings of the pumping station also demonstrate changing materials over the period: the 1854 and 1862 houses are of handmade bricks (commonly used until the end of the 1860s) whereas those built later are of machine-made bricks.

The waterworks closed in 1934 and the buildings now house the South Oxford Community Centre.

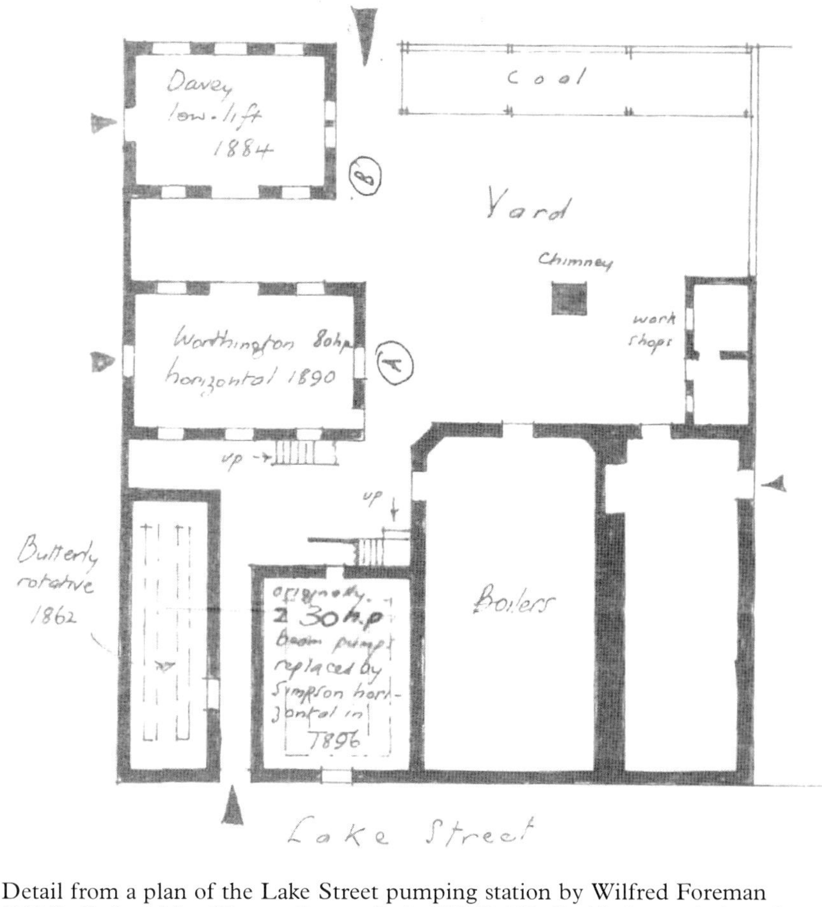

Detail from a plan of the Lake Street pumping station by Wilfred Foreman (1974). Oxfordshire History Centre. Ref: OXFO 352. By kind permission of Mrs. Sylvia Foreman.

This is the end of this walk. To return to the starting point, walk to the western end of Lake Street (which is a cul-de-sac) and turn left on to a footpath. Within a short distance turn right to cross the lake and then the railway lines on a raised walkway known as the Devil's Backbone. Beyond the railway sidings descend steep steps, continue along the path and over a footbridge. Shortly afterwards, turn right through a gateway and along a wide straight track laid out with concrete slabs down either side of it. Follow this track for three-quarters of a mile (1.2 km) through hay meadows. A bridge takes you over a stream; shortly afterwards cross another stream and then immediately turn right and follow the track which runs at right angles across the field towards the line of trees ahead. Emerge where the modern railway bridge crosses the river. Turn left along the towpath, crossing immediately a footbridge over Bulstake Stream. Continue along the footpath, past Osney Lock and back to the starting point of the walk.

Further Reading

William Page (ed.), *Victoria County History of Oxfordshire*, vol. 2, pp. 225–77: 'Industries' (1907).

Alan Crossley & C. R. Elrington (eds.), *Victoria County History of Oxfordshire*, vol. 4, *City of Oxford*, pp. 208–17: 'Economic History' and pp. 327–31: 'Mills and Fisheries' (1979).

Malcolm Graham, *On Foot in Oxford* (Oxford City Libraries Local History Collection, 1974–1988).

Malcolm Graham, *Images of Victorian Oxford* (Sutton, 1992).

Liz Woolley, 'Industrial Architecture in Oxford, 1870 to 1914', *Oxoniensia* 75 (2010).

Brigid Allen, *Morrell's of Oxford: the Family and their Brewery 1743–1993* (Oxfordshire Books, 1994).

James Bond & John Rhodes, *The Oxfordshire Brewer* (Oxfordshire Museum Services, 1985).

Brigid Allen, *Cooper's Oxford: A History of Frank Cooper Limited* (Archive Services of Oxford, 1989).

P. W. S. Andrews & E. Brunner, *The Eagle Ironworks Oxford: The Story of W. Lucy and Company Limited* (Mills & Boon, 1965).

T. Winckworth & M. Hobbs, *The Lucy Story: Portrait of a Family Company* (W. Lucy & Co. Ltd., 2009).

Mary Prior, *Fisher Row: Fishermen, Bargemen and Canal Boatmen, 1500–1900* (Clarendon Press, 1982).

Mark Davies & Catherine Robinson, *A Towpath Walk in Oxford: The Canal and River Thames between Wolvercote and the City* (Towpath Press, 2003).

Simon Wenham, 'Salter's of Oxford: a History of a Thames Boating Firm over a Century of Evolution (1858–*c.*1960)', *Oxoniensia* 71 (2006).

Laurence Waters, *Rail Centres: Oxford* (Booklaw, 2005).

Oxford Preservation Trust, LMS swing bridge project: www.oxfordpreservation.org.uk/projects/swingbridge.php

Local Heritage Organizations

There are a number of membership organizations which are concerned with Oxford's heritage and with making the city's historic sites more accessible and well known to the public:

The Oxford Preservation Trust (OPT) is committed to ensuring a positive future for Oxford, preserving and enhancing the city's historic character and green setting, while recognizing the needs of the 21st-century city. Members enjoy a programme of talks and guided walks around Oxford, free entry to Oxford Castle Unlocked and a regular newsletter. www.oxfordpreservation.org.uk

The Oxford Civic Society is concerned with the quality of Oxford's built environment and its impact on people's daily lives. The Society's priorities are to protect Oxford's heritage, to appreciate today's city, and to shape its future. Members enjoy talks, guided walks and visits in and around Oxford, and a regular newsletter. www.oxfordcivicsoc.org.uk

The Oxfordshire Architectural and Historical Society (OAHS) promotes the study and conservation of the county's archaeology and buildings. Members receive the society's journal *Oxoniensia* and can attend lectures and summer excursions. www.oahs.org.uk

The Oxfordshire Local History Association (OLHA) fosters and promotes the study and publication of local history and acts as an umbrella organization for local history groups, of which there are more than 80 in Oxfordshire. Members are kept in touch with local history research throughout the county via the Association's journal, newsletter, and regular study days. www.olha.org.uk

The Oxfordshire Buildings Record (OBR) aims to advance education and promote research on the buildings of Oxfordshire, to encourage the recording of historic buildings, and to create a publicly accessible repository of records. Members have access to training in the techniques used to record historic buildings and can participate in recording days, as well as receiving a regular newsletter. www.obr.org.uk

OXFORD'S WORKING PAST

A Tour of Victorian and Edwardian Industrial Buildings

Liz Woolley

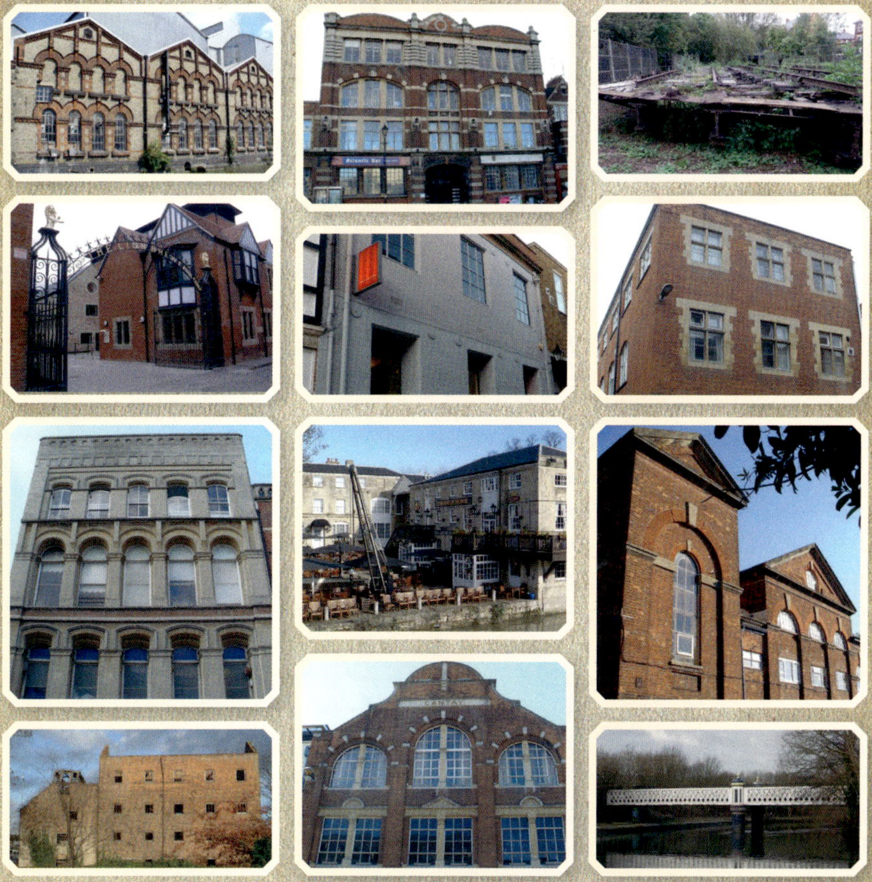

Also available from Huxley Scientific Press:

The Oxford Science Walk, by Sophie Huxley

Oxford Trees (2nd edn.), by Sophie Huxley

Darwin's Mysterious Illness, by Robert Youngson

Penicillin and Luck, by Norman Heatley

Eric Gill in Oxford, by Sophie Huxley

Aristotle, the Market Place, and the Idea of a University, by George Huxley

Forbidden Fruit, by Heathcote Williams

Transiting the Sun: Venus and the Key to the Size of the Cosmos, by John Woodruff

www.huxleyscientific.com